I0108370

MORE THAN MUD

Confidence, Imagination and Dreams

Kate Butler
BOOKS

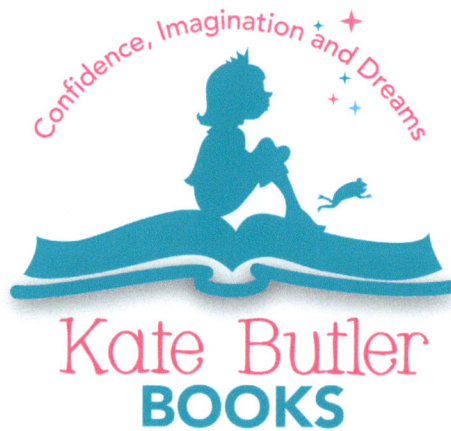

Copyright © 2013 Kate Butler
Library of Congress Control Number: 2014906833

www.katebutlerbooks.com

All rights reserved. No part of this book may be reproduced or transmitted in any form or by any means, electronic or mechanical, including photocopying, recording or by an information storage and retrieval system - except by a reviewer who may quote brief passages in a review to be printed in a magazine, newspaper or on the Web - without permission in writing from the author.

Back cover photo by Chele Conway
www.cheleconwayphotography.smugmug.com

Design and text layout by Margaret Cogswell
www.spiderbuddydesigns.com

To Ladybug and Lulu,

I will be forever grateful for each and every moment with you. You have taught me what love is. It is a privilege to be your mom.

. . . .

To Mel,

You are the best person I know.
Thank you for being you.

Once upon a time there was a girl named Maggie Mud. On the day Maggie was born her mommy felt magic and knew true love. On that day she made a promise to Maggie that no matter what happened in life, she would always keep things in perspective. Here is the story of how Maggie was taught to see **More Than Mud.**

Tonight your mommy tucks you in and kisses you goodnight. When you wake up with a cry, Mommy has magic ears that can hear you. Daddy still sleeps. Your big sister still sleeps. The dog still sleeps. But Mommy wakes up.

When Mommy comes into your room, she does not see a crying baby. She sees an angel. Mommy does not see a sleepless night; instead, she sees a little miracle.

Through your mommy's eyes, you are beautiful inside and out. By watching you, she learns what life is about.

Today you try peas for the first time. You love your first taste of food! You may play with more food than you eat but you have so much fun.

Mommy does not see a messy face. She sees a memory that she will cherish forever. Mommy can see your curiosity developing as you try something new.

This morning you ask if you can go outside and play. It rained yesterday, so you wear your raincoat and galoshes. You and your friends have a glorious time jumping through mud puddles!

Mommy does not see dirty clothes. She does not see icky shoes. Mommy sees **more than mud.** She sees creativity! Today you are a free spirit. Mommy sees the magnificence of your imagination.

Through your mommy's eyes, you are beautiful inside and out. By watching you, she learns what life is about.

Today Mommy finds that you have discovered her makeup drawer. Uh-oh!

But Mommy does not see eye shadow. She does not see blush. She does not see lipstick. All Mommy sees is your beauty radiating from within. For it is the light you have inside that shines the brightest. This is true beauty.

Tonight is your first ballet recital. As you plié and chassé across the stage, you look simply radiant! You twirl around in pure joy as you finally perform the routine you worked so hard to learn.

Mommy does not just see a dance routine.

A moment has stopped in time. She sees your confidence building.
Mommy sees you taking pride in your hard work. Mommy is
also very proud.

Through your mommy's eyes, you are beautiful inside and out.
By watching you, she learns what life is about.

Tonight is your first sleepover. You are so excited to spend the night at your best friend's house. You have plans to eat popcorn, watch movies, and stay up late.

But when it comes time to go to sleep, you feel scared and alone. Mommy comes to comfort you. There may be times when Mommy is not there, but Mommy's love will always be with you.

Tonight is your first school dance. Tonight you are nervous. You are not quite sure how to fix your hair. You worry that you may not have the perfect dress to wear.

Mommy has a different perspective. She does not see worry, but only your grace and strength. Mommy sees the difference you make in this world just by being you.

Through your mommy's eyes, you are beautiful inside and out. By watching you, she learns what life is about.

Today is your graduation day. As you walk across the stage, your family cheers for you. Hooray! Today we celebrate all of your success! Mommy sees more than a diploma.

She sees a future so very bright. She sees you dreaming big, without fear or limits. Mommy feels a sense of gratitude for the extraordinary person you have always been and continue to be.

Today you receive news that makes you feel very sad. The feelings you are experiencing bring tears to your eyes. Today you are asking, "Why?"

When Mommy sees your tears, she has tears too. But Mommy does not see all sadness; she also sees hope. As you find happiness again, you now know that all the love you will ever need has always been right inside of you.

Through your mommy's eyes, you are beautiful inside and out. By watching you, she learns what life is about.

Today is your wedding day. Mommy sees a blissful bride, but she also sees her little girl. She sees your big blue eyes looking up at her, just like the first time you ate peas. Mommy sees your beautiful spirit, the same spirit that jumped through the mud puddles.

Mommy sees through the perfect makeup and into a perfect soul. You light up the room, the same way you lit up the stage during your very first dance recital. You look angelic, just like the angel who woke up in the middle of the night so many years ago. When you were born, you became your mommy's miracle, and her miracle you will always be.

Many years from now, you will look through a mommy's eyes. On that day you will say, "Through your mommy's eyes, you are beautiful inside and out. By watching you, I will learn what life is all about."

There are many twists and turns in life. You have the power to decide how you react to every situation. You can choose to see mud, or you can choose to see **more than mud**. With a positive perspective, life becomes magical!

Always remember, you are perfect because you are you!

THE END

THE ENCHANTING WORLD OF MAGGIE MUD

Maggie is a young girl who loves tea parties, dress up and, of course, jumping in mud puddles! When Maggie and her friends jump around in the mud, they imagine they are in a magical princess world with fairies, magic sparkle dust and lots of candy. Maggie's dream is to grow up and become a Princess who rides horses and helps other people see **More Than Mud**. Maggie enjoys making new friends and getting to know new people just like YOU! Maggie would love for you to join her enchanting world where everyone can see "More Than Mud".

Would you like to be Maggie's friend?

Here are some ways you can connect with Maggie:

send maggie a letter

Share your "More Than Mud" Moment! When have you seen "More Than Mud"? Visit our website at **www.katebutlerbooks.com** where you can write to Maggie and submit your very own "More Than Mud" Moment.

maggie on WWW. the web!

Post or tweet your More Than Mud Moment!
Facebook Fan Page:
www.facebook.com/katebutlerbooks
Twitter: #katebutlerbooks
#MoreThanMudMoment
#MTMM

send maggie a picture

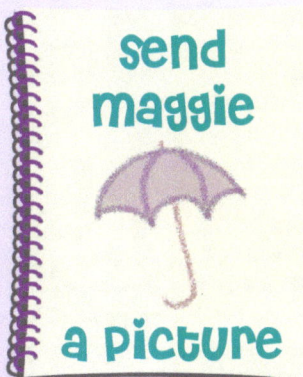

Visit **www.katebutlerbooks.com** to download your very own Maggie Mud coloring page. Maggie wants to see your artwork! Please mail to:

Kate Butler Books
157 Bridgeton Pike Suite #209
Mullica Hill, NJ 08062
Attention: Maggie Mud

DEVELOPMENTAL QUESTIONS

Has there been a time when you felt nervous? What has helped you relax?

Try teaching your child breathing techniques, meditations or calming exercises. These are all things that will be useful in years to come.

If anything were possible, what would your biggest dream be?

Secret: It is ALL possible! Create a Dream Board with your child.

What type of beauty do you have within?

Discuss how your child is: kind, grateful, helpful, caring, appreciative, respectful, generous.

Tell me about a time when you felt very proud of yourself.

Help them to feel proud of accomplishments that are tangible and acts of kindness that are intangible.

Was there a time when you felt scared or alone?

Discuss ways to help your child feel a sense of comfort. This is also a good opportunity to discuss how to avoid negative situations.

Tell me about a time you were curious about something and wanted to learn more.

Start a list with your child. Every week or month, explore something new that your child is curious about. Try something different! You may go on a nature walk, try a new recipe or go to the park where you can swing and talk together!

What have you used your imagination to create?

Provide a Dream Journal where your child's imagination can come alive!

Parent Challenge:
Next time it rains, take your child out to jump in mud puddles! This will be a memory that will be remembered for years to come.

About the Author

As a Certified Professional Success Coach (CPSC), Kate helps each client maximize their potential and reach goals beyond what they thought were possible...to Dream BIG! Kate is dedicated to inspiring others to believe in life and trust in themselves. She provides her clients with the tools to enhance the 8 essential areas of their lives: Finance, Relationships, Business, Personal Joy, Spiritual Growth, Environment, Wellness and Contribution. She believes that achieving true balance in these areas will bring focus and clarity to one's life purpose.

Kate has worked with hundreds of women, from stay-at-home moms to mompreneurs, to improve their businesses, relationships and happiness through her proven techniques. She prides herself on helping clients find internal peace and balance through her various coaching programs, which include 1 on 1 sessions, group retreats and monthly membership calls.

During 1 on 1 sessions, Kate coaches clients to first develop their dreams, then teaches them the tools needed to make those dreams a reality. Group retreats are a special way to connect, gain inspiration and feel empowered. The monthly membership calls are a flexible way for members to "dial in" to Kate on a monthly basis for insight and support in defining their purpose or to elevate their lives through personal development. Clients have experienced life changing results in their marriages, businesses and finances. Kate's goal is to inspire and empower clients to believe that in life, anything and everything is possible when you **Dream BIG!**

Kate would love to hear from you. To offer thoughts or to connect with Kate, please email her directly at kate@katebutlerbooks.com.

"More Than" SERIES

Find out more by visiting her website at: www.katebutlerbooks.com

www.ingramcontent.com/pod-product-compliance
Lightning Source LLC
Chambersburg PA
CBHW041553040426
42447CB00002B/169

9 780999 360026